Pod Digs a Pit

Written by Clare Helen Welsh

Illustrated by Michael Emmerson

Collins

Pod digs! Pod digs!

Pod digs a pit.

Pod digs! Pod digs!

It is a tin.

Pod digs! Pod digs!

It is a dog.

Pod digs! Pod digs!

It is a top!

Pod digs! Tap! Tap!

It is a pot!

11

Pod sits. Pod sits.

It is a map!

14

 # After reading

Letters and Sounds: Phase 2

Word count: 48

Focus phonemes: /g/ /o/

Common exception word: is

Curriculum links: Understanding the World: People and Communities; The World

Early learning goals: Reading: read and understand simple sentences; use phonic knowledge to decode regular words and read them aloud accurately; read some common irregular words; demonstrate understanding when talking with others about what they have read

Developing fluency

- Encourage your child to sound talk and then blend the words, e.g. /d/o/g/. It may help to point to each sound as your child reads.
- Then ask your child to reread the sentence to support fluency and understanding.
- You could reread the whole book to your child to model fluency and rhythm in the story.

Phonic practice

- Ask your child to sound talk and blend each of the following words:
  d/i/g/s   P/o/d   d/o/g   t/o/p
- Can your child find the word that has both a /g/ and an /o/ sound in it? (*dog*)
- Look at the "I spy sounds" pages (14–15). Discuss the picture with your child. Can they find items/ examples of words containing the /g/ sound? (*gold, globe, garlic, goat, grass, gorilla, grapes, green, gloves, gift, glue, golf, grandad, guitar, glasses, gecko*)

Extending vocabulary

- Ask your child:
  - On page 10, Pod finds the pot. It makes a **tap, tap** sound. Can you think of any other words to describe the sound? (e.g. *bang, ping, knock, pop, ting*)
  - On page 5, Pod finds a **tin**. A tin is a type of container. Can you think of any other containers? (e.g. *a can, a box, a bowl, a bottle*)